GREAT ESCAPES

THE IRISH POTATO FAMINE

Dennis Brindell Fradin

This publication represents the opinions and views of the author based on Dennis Brindell Fradin's personal experience, knowledge, and research. The information in this book serves as a general guide only. The author and publisher have used their best efforts in preparing this book and disclaim liability rising directly and indirectly from the use and application of this book.

Other Marshall Cavendish Offices:
Marshall Cavendish International (Asia) Private Limited, 1 New Industrial Road, Singapore 536196 • Marshall Cavendish International (Thailand) Co Ltd. 253 Asoke, 12th Flr, Sukhumvit 21 Road, Klongtoey Nua, Wattana, Bangkok 10110, Thailand • Marshall Cavendish (Malaysia) Sdn Bhd, Times Subang, Lot 46, Subang Hi-Tech Industrial Park, Batu Tiga, 40000 Shah Alam, Selangor Darul Ehsan, Malaysia

Marshall Cavendish is a trademark of Times Publishing Limited
All websites were available and accurate when this book was sent to press.

Library of Congress Cataloging-in-Publication Data

Fradin, Dennis B.
The Irish potato famine / by Dennis Fradin.
p. cm. — (Great escapes)
Summary: "Provides comprehensive information on the history leading up to the Irish potato famine, presents accounts of narrow escapes, and discusses the legacy of the event"—Provided by publisher.
Includes bibliographical references and index.
ISBN 978-1-60870-473-6 (print)   ISBN 978-1-60870-694-5 (ebook)
1. Ireland—History—Famine, 1845-1852—Juvenile literature. 2. Escapes--Ireland—History—19th century—Juvenile literature. 3. Disaster victims—Ireland—History—19th century—Juvenile literature. 4. Irish—Migrations—History—19th century—Juvenile literature. 5. Ireland—Emigration and immigration—History—19th century—Juvenile literature. I. Title.
DA950.7.F73 2012
941.5081—dc22
2010018788

Senior Editor: Deborah Grahame-Smith
Publisher: Michelle Bisson
Art Director: Anahid Hamparian
Series Designer: Kay Petronio
Photo research by Linda Sykes

The photographs in this book are used by permission and through the courtesy of: New Walk Museum & Art Gallery, Leicester, UK/Photo ©Leicester Arts & Museums/ The Bridgeman Art Library: cover; ©Geray Sweeney/Corbis: 1; Trustees of the Watts Gallery, Compton, Surrey, UK/The Bridgeman Art Library: 4; The Granger Collection: 8, 19, 21, 27; Archive Photos/Getty Images: 10; ©Holger Burmeister/Alamy: 12; Courtesy of the National Library of Ireland: 14; ©World History/Topham/The Image Works: 18; ©Mary Evans Picture Library/Grosvenor Prints/The Image Works: 23; Hulton Archive/Getty Images: 25, 59; Mary Evans Picture Library: 29, 49; Private Collection/The Bridgeman Art Library: 31; Northwind Picture Archives: 34; Archive Images/fotosearch/Getty Images: 40; Library of Congress: 44; ©Christian Kober/Robert Harding World Imagery/ Corbis: 53; Robert Knudsen/White House photo/John F. Kennedy Presidential Library and Museum, Boston: 54; Library of Congress: 56; ©Patrick Durand/Sygma/Corbis: 62.

Printed in Malaysia (T)
135642

CONTENTS

Introduction: "Living, Walking Ghosts"....... 4

ONE: The Roots of the Famine............. 8

TWO: The Irish Potato Famine............ 16

THREE: Escape from the Great Famine 34

FOUR: The Irish Diaspora 44

FIVE: Meanwhile, Back in Ireland.......... 56

Time Line............................... 64

Notes................................... 66

Glossary 72

Further Information 75

Bibliography........................... 76

Index................................... 77

Irish peasant families, who relied on the potato to sustain them from one harvest to the next, were devastated by the famine.

INTRODUCTION

"LIVING, WALKING GHOSTS"

The year was 1846, and the European country of Ireland was in the midst of a famine—a period of widespread and intense hunger. The people who experienced it called the occurrence *An Gorta Mor*, which means "the Great Hunger" in Gaelic, the ancient Irish language. In English the disaster is known as the Irish Potato Famine because the food that many people depended on was not fit to eat. A fungus had caused a blight that infected potato crops and destroyed harvests throughout Ireland.

Asenath Nicholson, a teacher from Vermont, was among the many volunteers who tried to ease the suffering in Ireland. From 1846 to 1848 Nicholson was a one-woman relief corps. In addition to baking and passing out bread, she operated a soup kitchen in Dublin, Ireland's capital city. A devout Quaker, she also wanted to share her interpretation of the Bible with Irish Catholics. She trekked across the countryside and aided the hungry wherever she could. In her book *Annals of the Famine in Ireland*, Nicholson describes some of her encounters with the "living, walking ghosts," as she calls the famine victims.

While staying at a friend's home near Dublin, Nicholson encountered some men who were working as road builders to earn a few pennies for their families. She took particular note of one man who was so "sick with fever" that "he staggered with his spade" as he worked. "Reader," Nicholson writes,

> if you have never seen a starving human being, may you never! In my
>
> childhood I had been frightened with the stories of ghosts, . . . but imagination
>
> had come short of the sight of this man. . . . [He] was emaciated to the last degree;
>
> he was tall, his eyes prominent, his skin shriveled.

For a few days, Nicholson provided food for the tall man with protruding eyes and for several other road workers who came to the door of her friend's home. She learned that the tall man received only fifteen pennies per day to build roads from

THE POOR PEOPLE OF IRELAND

Even before the Great Famine, many Irish people suffered terrible poverty. In 1835, Frenchman Alexis de Tocqueville described the way poor Irish people lived: "Walls of mud, roofs of thatch, one room. No chimney, smoke goes out the door. The pig lies in the middle of the house . . . the population looks very wretched. Many wear clothes with holes or much patched. Most of them are bare-headed and barefoot."

sunup to sundown. All the men were enduring hunger and hard times, but the man with protruding eyes was especially struggling to save his wife, their six children, and himself from starvation. Fifteen pennies a day didn't go very far for a family of six, so, as he told Nicholson, he had been forced to sell or pawn most of his family's clothing.

Nicholson soon ran out of provisions and had to turn away the hungry road workers who came to the door. "We must die of the hunger, God be praised!" said the tall man with protruding eyes. He and the other road builders gave Nicholson their blessing and walked away.

Several days passed, and Nicholson neither saw nor heard anything about the tall man. What had happened to him? What had become of his wife and their six children? Had the famine claimed him and his family as it had so many thousands of others? Or had they perhaps escaped Ireland for a new life in America, Australia, or beyond?

One farmer in western Ireland reported sticking a spade in the ground and finding that the potatoes unearthed had turned to mud inside.

THE ROOTS OF THE FAMINE

People first lived in Ireland at least ten thousand years ago. Ireland's earliest residents moved around while they fished and hunted. Several thousand years ago, ancient Irish people learned to grow crops and raise livestock. Farming enabled them to put down roots and build settlements.

Around 400 BCE, a people called the Celts traveled to Ireland by boat from other parts of Europe. The Celts and their culture spread throughout the Emerald Isle, as Ireland is nicknamed. For example, the Celts brought their language, Gaelic, to Ireland. To this day, people in Ireland speak Irish Gaelic, often simply called Irish.

Christianity arrived in Ireland during the 400s CE. Around 405 CE, a raiding party kidnapped a Christian youth named Patrick in England and took him to Ireland as a slave. After six years of slavery, he escaped and made his way home. However, he hoped to return to Ireland one day to preach to the people about Christianity.

After studying to be a priest, Patrick got his wish when the pope sent him to Ireland. While traveling around the Emerald Isle, Patrick taught the Irish people about Christianity and reportedly established three hundred churches. Today, Irish people around the world celebrate the day of his death—March 17—as Saint Patrick's Day.

The English Take Over

In 1171, King Henry II of England and his army seized control of Ireland. This began more than seven centuries of British rule and sowed the seeds of the Great Famine. During the 1550s, England began a colonization scheme called the plantation of

Legend says Saint Patrick drove the snakes from Ireland—though actual snakes probably never lived there.

POTATO HISTORY

Potatoes are so closely associated with Ireland that people often assume potatoes originated there. Actually, potatoes seem to have come from South America, where they grew wild as many as 13,000 years ago. At least five thousand years ago, ancient farmers began planting and growing potatoes.

Explorers returning from the New World brought potatoes to Europe in the late 1500s. English explorer Sir Walter Raleigh reportedly introduced potatoes to the Emerald Isle by planting them on his Irish property in the 1580s.

Ireland. Irish families were evicted from their property, while British settlers were "planted," or sent to live on these lands. Native Irish people often had to work for the new British landlords or move to less fertile land.

Gradually England took over more and more of Ireland. By the mid-1600s, British landlords controlled 80 percent of the country. By the 1770s, landlords loyal to England held around 95 percent of Ireland.

The desire for land wasn't the only reason why English leaders wanted to rule Ireland. Another issue involved religion. The Irish and the English were both predominantly Christian. However, the Irish were Catholics, while the English were Protestants. English officials wanted to stamp out Catholicism in their Irish colony.

Over the years, English legislators enacted a series of laws, known as Penal Laws, in persecution of Irish Catholics. Catholic worship was outlawed, so Irish Catholics practiced

Ancient Celtic crosses, dating back one thousand years, are among the oldest Christian relics in Ireland. As the new religion grew, Celtic gods became the heroes of Irish folklore.

their faith by holding services in secluded places. Since Catholic schools were also outlawed, many Irish children attended Protestant schools or had no formal education. Some attended "hedge schools"—Catholic schools that met secretly outdoors.

In addition, Irish Catholics couldn't vote or hold public office. They weren't allowed to become teachers or to practice law. It was also illegal for Catholics in Ireland to own a gun, to buy property, or to own a horse valued at more than 5 pounds.

At times, the Irish people rebelled against English rule. The odds were against the Irish rebels, for England was the world's most powerful country. Besides, less than 100 miles (160 kilometers) of sea separated Ireland and England. English soldiers could be sent over quickly with little difficulty.

Although the rebellions failed, England's leaders realized that something must be done about Ireland. In 1801, England established the United Kingdom of Great Britain and Ireland. The name made it sound like England and Ireland had become equals, but they hadn't. Although they comprised three-fourths of Ireland's population, Catholics were still mistreated. For example, laws restricted their ownership of land, and certain jobs were closed to them. Furthermore, only Protestants could represent Ireland in the British parliament, the United Kingdom's lawmaking body in London, England.

People began growing potatoes in Ireland sometime between 1585 and 1600. Ireland had excellent potato-growing conditions: moist, cool air and deep soil that crumbled easily. At first Irish farmers grew potatoes to supplement their main diet of oats, other grains, and dairy products. However, potatoes soon proved advantageous over other foods. They had great nutritional value. Potatoes were also inexpensive, and it was easy to grow them in large quantities.

Each year, potatoes became a more important food in Ireland. In 1845, the country's population was 9 million. By then, potatoes were a vital part of the diet—and often were the *only* food for two-thirds of Ireland's population. On average, adults in Ireland ate 10 pounds of potatoes per day!

There was a drawback to depending on potatoes as the main or only source of food. Now and then the potato crop spoiled or died. There were several causes for this. Sometimes the ground froze, and the plants were ruined. Droughts (periods of insufficient rain) sometimes dried out the potatoes, which normally consist of 80 percent water. Other times, heavy rain

A view of the village of Loughrea in 1849. That year, 212,000 people left Ireland to escape the famine. Most headed for the United States.

drowned the potato crops. Insect enemies could harm potatoes, as could fungi, viruses, and bacterial infections. Between 1800 and 1844 alone, the potato crop failed in one part of Ireland or another in twenty-two different years—half the time.

If a country depends heavily on one crop for food, a poor harvest can lead to widespread hunger. Potato crop failures have caused many famines in Ireland. But starvation isn't the only way famines claim lives. People who are deprived of food for long periods become weak and subject to disease. Starvation and disease have claimed thousands of lives at a time—mostly poor Catholic families—during famines in Ireland.

Usually, the failure of the potato crop occurred in just portions of Ireland. Most of the country still produced healthy potatoes. Then, in 1845, the potato crop failure was so huge that it resulted in the disaster known as the Great Famine.

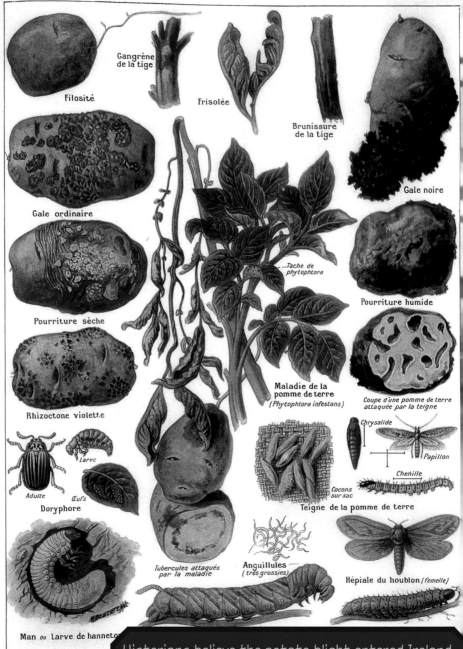

Filosité

Gangrène de la tige

Frisolée

Brunissure de la tige

Gale noire

Gale ordinaire

Tache de phytophtora

Pourriture humide

Pourriture sèche

Rhizoctone violette

Maladie de la pomme de terre
(Phytophtora infestans)

Coupe d'une pomme de terre attaquée par la teigne

Chrysalide

Papillon

Larve

Chenille

Adulte   Œufs
Doryphore

Cocons sur sac

Teigne de la pomme de terre

Tubercules attaqués par la maladie

Anguillules (très grossies)

Hépiale du houblon (femelle)

Man ou Larve de hanneton

Historians believe the potato blight entered Ireland aboard a ship from the United States. To make matters worse, a drought struck Ireland and most of Europe during the time of the Great Famine.

THE IRISH POTATO FAMINE

One of the worst disasters of the nineteenth century was caused by a tiny organism with a big name: *Phytophthora infestans.* It was a fungus, the category of organisms that includes mushrooms as well as bread molds. In potatoes, *Phytophthora infestans* causes a disease known as late blight. Dark spots and furry growths form on the potato plants' leaves. After that, the leaves and stems of the potato plants decay. The plants die, and the parts that people usually eat—called the *tubers*—turn into inedible, dark masses of pulp.

Someone noticed late blight on potato plants at Dublin's Botanic Gardens in August 1845. On September 13, botanist John Lindley of the University of London wrote the following announcement in the *Gardeners' Chronicle*:

> We stop the press, with very great regret, to announce that the potato [blight] has . . . declared itself in Dublin. The crops about Dublin are suddenly perishing. . . . [W]here will Ireland be, in the event of a universal potato rot?

The answer to Dr. Lindley's question was that Ireland would be in severe trouble—for a much longer period of time than earlier famines. In 1845, nearly half of Ireland's potato crop was lost to the blight. The situation worsened in 1846, when the blight destroyed nearly 80 percent of the potato crop. In 1847, *Phytophthora infestans* ruined one-third of the potato crop. In 1848, the blight killed half the country's potatoes.

Farmers who lost their potato crop still had to pay rent to their landlords. Families who couldn't pay their rent were thrown off their lands. To make sure the poor families didn't come back, landlords often "tumbled," or knocked down, their tenants' little homes. Historian Cecil Woodham-Smith described the mass destruction of poor farmers' homes in the town of Ballinglass in 1846:

> . . . the houses were then demolished—roofs torn off, walls thrown down. The scene was frightful; women running, wailing with pieces of their property and clinging to door-posts from which they had to be forcibly torn; men cursing, children screaming with fright. That night the people slept in the ruins; next day they were driven out, the foundations of the houses were torn up and razed, and no neighbor was allowed to take them in.

The people whose huts and cabins were tumbled usually had nowhere else to live. Many of them simply dug a deep hole in the ground and built a roof over it with sticks and patches of turf. This burrow, which was called a scalp, provided little protection against rain and cold.

As thousands of families who grew little or nothing besides potatoes ran out of food, hunger set in across much of Ireland. The resulting famine grew worse with time. People became so desperate that they wandered around the countryside in search

After their small cottages were tumbled down by British landlords, Irish families were forced to live in a burrow, or scalp.

THE DAY AFTER THE EJECTMENT.

of something to eat. They devoured blackberries and dandelion roots, and when those were gone they ate weeds, grass, and the leaves and bark of trees.

The victims of the Great Famine left behind few written descriptions. This is almost always the case when a famine occurs. For one thing, starving people are often unable or unwilling to make a written record of their suffering. Also, famines usually affect a country's poorest and least educated people. The victims of the Irish Potato Famine were mainly poor and uneducated Catholics who had never learned to read and write.

HUNGER & THIRST

Human beings can live without food for about four weeks. In some instances people can survive for as long as six weeks without food. Water is a different story. The human body, which is about two-thirds water, can survive for only about four days without replenishing its supply of this vital fluid.

A number of officials and relief workers who witnessed the Great Famine did leave written records, however. William Forster, a minister who investigated the famine for a group of Quakers from England, wrote that the starving children resembled "skeletons, their features sharpened with hunger and their limbs wasted, so that there was little left but bones. . . . [T]he happy expression of infancy gone from their faces, leaving the anxious look of premature old age."

In her book *Annals of the Famine of Ireland*, Asenath Nicholson describes a horrifying incident that she experienced in the western part of the country:

A cabin was seen closed one day a little out of the town when [a friend of mine] had the curiosity to open it, and in a dark corner he found a family of the father, mother, and two children, lying in close compact. [T]he mother, it appeared, had died last, and probably fastened the door, which was always the custom when all hope was extinguished, to get into the darkest corner and die where passers-by could not see them. . . . The [friend] called, begging me to look in. I did not, and could not endure, as the famine progressed, such sights. . . . [T]hey were too real. . . . [T]he horror of meeting living, walking ghosts, or stumbling upon the dead in my path at night, inclined me to keep [indoors] when necessity did not call.

A family cooks their meager fare over a fire on an earth floor. The Irish had difficulty grinding and cooking the Indian corn and meal Britain purchased for them from the United States.

What about the tall man Nicholson had fed while visiting her friend near Dublin? A few days after she ran out of provisions, Nicholson received money from New York to help famine victims. She immediately went out and purchased large quantities of cornmeal, bread, and milk. Hoping that the tall man was still among the living, she sent word for him to come and get food. When he arrived, her first impression was that he was "sinking" toward death, but the food she supplied saved his life and the lives of a few other starving road builders.

Famine-Related Diseases Claim Huge Tolls

In most famines, far more people die of disease than of starvation. Extreme hunger weakens people to the point where they lack the strength to fight off a large array of illnesses. Researchers estimate that for every person who starved to death in the Irish Potato Famine, nine people died of diseases associated with the lack of food.

Typhus, a disease transmitted by microorganisms that enter a victim's body through lice, claimed a huge toll during the Great Famine. The victims' skin turned dark, and they vomited and ran a fever. In severe cases patients became delirious, their limbs thrashed about, and their ordeal ended in death. According to Ireland's 1851 census, typhus epidemics claimed nearly 200,000 lives between 1846 and 1850.

In some areas people established "fever hospitals" for patients with such illnesses as typhus and relapsing fever, another infectious disease spread by lice. Some of these so-called hospitals were really just sheds where doctors tried to comfort the sick and dying. Hundreds of doctors and Catholic priests who came into contact with contagious patients became ill themselves. In the province of Munster in southern Ireland, forty-eight doctors died within about a year. Most died of fevers they had developed while treating patients.

Dysentery, an irritation of the intestines caused by microorganisms, was another major killer. Spread through contaminated food and water, dysentery causes intestinal pain and other digestive problems. Dysentery killed 25,000 people in Ireland in 1847 alone. The following year, cholera, another intestinal disease spread by contaminated water and food, broke out in Ireland. Before subsiding in 1850, the cholera epidemic claimed at least 30,000 lives.

Dublin Hospital. Most "fever hospitals" were not this grand, but were often makeshift structures in which victims of typhus, cholera, and other deadly diseases were treated.

Response—or Lack of Response— to the Crisis

Many historians blame England for creating the conditions that allowed the Irish Potato Famine to occur. In his 1860 book *The Last Conquest of Ireland (Perhaps),* Irish journalist John Mitchel writes, "The Almighty, indeed, sent the potato blight but the English created the Famine." In 1993, historian Dennis Clark wrote that the famine was "the culmination of generations of neglect, misrule, and repression. It was an epic of colonial cruelty." Had the Irish been in charge of their own lands and nation over the centuries, farmers might have learned to grow other crops besides potatoes. Then, if the potato crop had failed, families would still have had other food to eat.

The question was, what would the English do to help now that the disaster was under way? In the 1840s, England was the world's leading industrial nation and head of the richest and most powerful empire on Earth. It would be very costly, but England had the resources to send massive amounts of food, as well as doctors and nurses, to Ireland.

Some British leaders wanted England to do whatever was needed to save lives. The Earl of Clarendon warned that only England's might could end the famine and that "Ireland cannot be left to her own resources." Edward Twisleton, a British official who helped with relief measures in Ireland, declared that unless they did their best to combat the famine, English lawmakers would be "slowly murdering the peasantry."

Most British lawmakers favored granting Ireland minimal aid, however. One reason was the popularity of an economic theory called *laissez-faire*. Laissez-faire is a French phrase roughly meaning "let it alone." Its supporters claim that, in the long run, a country's people will find better ways to solve problems than politicians will, so the government should keep its hands off a nation's monetary affairs. Supporters of laissez-faire believe that merchants and businesses should make their own decisions rather than deferring to government regulations.

There were other reasons why England didn't do more to combat the Irish Potato Famine. For one thing, most of the victims were Catholic, and prejudice against Irish Catholics was still widespread in England. Also, English lawmakers weren't eager to help a country that had been so rebellious in recent decades. The role of landlords was also a factor. Many

CHARLES TREVELYAN

Charles Trevelyan (1807–1886) was born in Taunton, England. His gift for languages helped him win appointments to important posts in British-controlled India starting at age nineteen. Then, in 1840, Trevelyan returned to London, where he served as assistant treasury secretary for nearly twenty years. As the man in charge of aiding Irish Potato Famine victims, Trevelyan did little, apparently because he was prejudiced against the Irish and their religion. In fact, he visited Ireland just once during the entire famine. Yet his fellow Englishmen approved of the job he had done, and in 1848 he was knighted as *Sir* Charles Trevelyan for his services in Ireland.

landlords saw the famine as an opportunity to clear their land of tenants and convert the land for grazing sheep or cattle.

Many British people became increasingly unwilling to assist the Irish as the famine continued. Lord John Russell was the United Kingdom's prime minister during the Great Famine. Making it clear that England would not rescue Ireland, Prime Minister Russell declared, "We cannot feed the [Irish] people."

Assistant Treasury Secretary Charles Trevelyan was the British official in charge of helping Ireland during the Great Potato Famine. Trevelyan seemed to feel that the Irish people deserved what was happening to them. In his 1848 book *The Irish Crisis*, Trevelyan refers to the famine as "the judgement of God on an indolent and unself-reliant people." Making the disaster sound like a divine punishment, he ends his book by calling the famine "a direct stroke of an all-wise . . . Providence."

The bottom line was that England provided aid for Ireland, but not nearly enough. During the famine the British government sent 10 million pounds to assist Ireland. This amount equaled about 50 million American dollars. That may sound like a fortune, yet it wasn't nearly enough to feed or to heal the millions of men, women, and children who needed help. And Ireland was expected to repay most of the 10 million pounds, which England issued as a loan.

Fever hospitals, a key part of the effort to control epidemics during the famine, treated 600,000 patients between 1847 and 1850. However, these hospitals were often so crowded that several patients occupied a single bed, and some patients had to stay on the streets. Furthermore, the fever hospitals were often so dirty that epidemics tended to spread rather than to end there.

"Appalling, awful, heart sickening" was the way a visitor described the fever hospital in Bantry, County Cork. Fever

A grim but common scene was that of workers and their carts collecting the dead from ditches, huts, and fields for burial.

patients—both living and dead—lay side by side on the straw-covered floor. There was no medicine and not even any water for patients to drink. The hospital's only doctor was ill, and there was just one nurse, whom the visitor called "utterly unfit" to tend the patients.

In addition to fever hospitals, 130 workhouses, commonly called poorhouses, had been built in Ireland by 1847. In these buildings, famine victims who had nowhere else to go could get something to eat and a place to sleep. In return, workhouse residents who were strong enough were expected to grind corn and to do other tasks.

Famine victims generally loathed the workhouses and dreaded having to go there, for it meant that they could no longer care for themselves. Besides, workhouses were overcrowded and had such terrible conditions that many people never got out alive. In some towns, one building doubled as both a workhouse and a fever hospital. In 1847, in the town of Fermoy in County Cork, two thousand people, both sick and well, were packed into a building designed to hold eight hundred. Disease spread, and within two months about 550 people—more than a quarter of the residents—died in the Fermoy workhouse.

Visitors to the workhouses were especially sad to witness the plight of children. At the workhouse in Bandon, County Cork, a visitor to the children's section counted 102 boys occupying 24 beds, with as many as 6 boys to a single bed. The filth in the workhouse was "revolting," the visitor added, and a "disgusting stench lasts all day." A visitor to a County Galway workhouse reported to his wife, "It was enough to have broken the stoutest heart to have seen the poor little children in the union workhouse yesterday—their flesh hanging so loose from their little bones."

Irish Potato Famine victims generally preferred outdoor relief, a government program, to living in the crowded, disease-ridden workhouses. Through outdoor relief, able-bodied men, as well as some women and children, could live at home while working on road- and bridge-building projects. Outdoor workers labored twelve hours a day, six days a week. They received small salaries that varied with the amount of work they did. The idea was that outdoor workers would earn money to buy food for their families rather than receiving it as a gift.

When Asenath Nicholson began helping the tall road builder with protruding eyes, he was working in an outdoor relief program. The tall man was a living example of how the system didn't work well. To start with, paying outdoor workers according to how much they accomplished wasn't as fair as it sounds. It meant that those who most needed

A ship from New York brings provisions for famine victims to Ireland's ports. Eventually, ships would leave those ports and take the Irish to new lands as the famine continued.

help—people weakened by hunger and illness—earned the least money. For instance, the tall road builder earned only fifteen British pennies a day—equivalent to about thirty U.S. cents. A family of eight couldn't survive on that amount. One day Nicholson learned that one of the tall road builder's six children had died because of a lack of food and medical care. Nicholson had observed that the tall man was so "sick with fever" that he "staggered" about. Yet the government did little to help such families.

Some historians claim that Ireland actually had enough farm products to feed all its people during the Great Potato Famine. In each year of the famine, a portion of the potato crop was salvaged. Some Irish farmers also produced oats and other food products.

The problem was that Ireland's richer people—including the English landowners—produced much of this food. These wealthy people sold their farm products to markets in England and America for a handsome price. The British parliament could have made it illegal to take these food products out of Ireland, but that would have cut into the English landlords' profits. So while people were starving in Ireland, ships packed with food were sailing out of the country to foreign ports.

Help from America and Other Countries

The crisis in Ireland drew a great deal of attention from around the world. Hundreds of organizations and individuals sent money and food to Ireland. Some people journeyed thousands of miles to offer aid in person, just as many Irish folks were trying to leave Ireland. By the early 1840s, more immigrants were emigrating to the United States from

HELP FROM AMERICAN INDIANS

A small but heartfelt contribution to Ireland came from an American Indian tribe. In the early 1830s, the Choctaw had been forced to move from their Mississippi homelands to Oklahoma. Thousands of Choctaw had died on the journey, which the survivors called the Trail of Tears. Having known hardship and oppression themselves, the Choctaw scraped together $710 to aid the Irish Potato Famine victims.

A Quaker soup house. Meals of soup and bread were free; people were only required to bring their own bowls.

Ireland than from any other country, and several million Americans were at least partially of Irish heritage. U.S. organizers held big fund-raising campaigns for the famine victims. Together the cities of New York, Philadelphia, and Baltimore raised more than a million dollars, equal to over $25 million today. In addition, American aid workers gathered food and clothing and loaded it onto the *Jamestown* on St. Patrick's Day—March 17, 1847. Volunteers then sailed the vessel across the Atlantic Ocean and delivered the supplies to Ireland.

Although people criticized the British government for not doing enough during the famine, many English people

LOCOMOTIVES, VOLCANOES, AND BIRD DROPPINGS

Some people had strange, unscientific theories about the causes of the Irish Potato Famine. One idea was that static electricity generated by train locomotives had brought on the potato blight. Another theory was that volcanoes deep inside the earth were belching out vapors that killed the potatoes. Yet another idea was that bird droppings, which some farmers used as fertilizer, were ruining the potato crop.

contributed to Irish relief. For example, in 1847, Jewish banker Lionel de Rothschild founded the British Relief Association to aid starving people in Ireland. Composed of British bankers and businessmen, the association helped feed 200,000 Irish children each day.

India was one of the first foreign countries to come forward. Soon after the disaster began, the Indian Relief Fund raised 14,000 pounds for the famine victims. That was equal to $70,000 at the time and would be equivalent to nearly $2 million today. Donations also came from Scotland, Wales, Turkey, Russia, Canada, Argentina, Venezuela, Australia, and South Africa.

Religious groups from around the world helped Ireland as well. Quakers in England and the United States sent large sums of money. Some Quakers traveled to poverty-stricken areas of Ireland to open soup houses and to distribute farm equipment and seeds. Catholics, Jews, and Protestant groups from many lands also sent money.

By late 1847, the Great Potato Famine had been devastating Ireland for two years. Some people were eating frogs and rats to survive. Yet at the end of 1847, Charles Trevelyan made a surprising announcement. Despite the fact that hunger and disease were still claiming thousands of lives, he announced the famine was over. In 1848, the British government also declared that the famine had ended. In truth, however, the Irish Potato Famine still had four years to go.

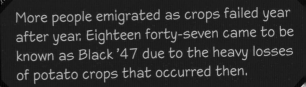

More people emigrated as crops failed year after year. Eighteen forty-seven came to be known as Black '47 due to the heavy losses of potato crops that occurred then.

THREE

ESCAPE FROM THE GREAT FAMINE

The British government had a reason to declare the Irish Potato Famine over in 1848. Parliament was reducing the amount of money it was spending on Ireland, and English politicians wanted the world to think the crisis was ending. Lawmakers wanted to shift responsibility for assisting famine victims to Ireland's rich landowners by levying taxes.

Despite the government's announcement, the potato blight struck again in 1849 and 1850. Deaths from starvation and disease continued. Most historians say that the Irish Potato Famine lasted seven years, from 1845 to 1852.

As time passed, newspaper reporters lost interest in the Great Famine and its seemingly endless cycle of blight, hunger, and epidemics. Consequently, it is difficult to find details about the later years of the famine. Remaining resources include stories that survivors told and passed along for generations before someone wrote them down.

For example, County Limerick residents told of a widow who walked 10 miles (16 km) to the market and bought flour. Someone stole her flour, so she continued on another 10 miles (16 km) to purchase two loaves of bread and a little milk. By the time she arrived home and gave the bread and milk to her famished child, she had walked 40 miles (64 km).Other stories such as this one, related by a County Roscommon native, were gruesome:

> My father, who was also named Johnny Callaghan, was a baker during the Famine years in the workhouse [at] Castlerea, County Roscommon. I was a young lad assisting my father. In the bakehouse my father and I were engaged all day baking. My father was always nervous to appear in public with flour dust on his clothes, so ravenous were some people he feared they would attack and kill him [trying to eat the flour dust]. Seeing people die of hunger was awful but it could not equal seeing them die of cholera. On the road leading to the workhouse a son was wheeling his father, dying of cholera, on a wheel barrow. On reaching the workhouse the father was dead and the son collapsed and died in a few hours time.

Thousands of people like Johnny Callaghan witnessed terrible scenes of death. The Irish Potato Famine took a huge toll. Just before the famine began in 1845, Ireland's population was 9 million. By 1852, when the famine was ending, the population had dropped to 6.5 million. It is very unusual for a country to lose 2.5 million people so quickly.

Approximately one million of those people died in the famine—900,000 through disease and 100,000 through starvation. This number of fatalities makes the Great Irish Potato Famine one of the deadliest catastrophes Europe has ever suffered.

Leaving Ireland

What about the other million and a half people who disappeared from Ireland between 1845 and 1852? They decided to leave Ireland and move to other lands. Some were so desperate to escape the famine that they committed crimes so they would be sent to Australia—a punishment known as transportation. Australia was a British penal colony at that time.

For example, at Westport in County Mayo, seventeen-year-old Dominic Ginelly was found guilty of stealing ropes. Insisting that he wasn't sorry for his crime, Ginelly asked to be transported. He got his wish and was shipped to Australia for seven years. The Ruddy brothers—eight-year-old John, twelve-year-old Austin, and fifteen-year-old Charles Ruddy, from Clare Island in County Mayo—were pronounced guilty of stealing sheep. They, too, were delighted to be sentenced to live in Australia for seven years. When asked if he knew what transportation was, another convicted youth, Owen Eady, said that it meant he wouldn't starve to death.

Most people who departed Ireland did so the traditional way. They scraped together enough money to buy a one-way ship ticket. Several thousand Irish people sailed to Australia, more than 10,000 miles (16,000 km) from the Emerald Isle. About 200,000 people made the 100-mile (160-km) voyage to England, where they settled in Liverpool and other cities. They were mainly very poor Irish people who despised England but could afford only a short trip.

The United States was by far the most popular destination of the Irish Potato Famine refugees. Long before the famine, Irish people had settled in North America and had helped the colonies achieve independence from England. Like other ethnic groups, people of Irish heritage considered America the land of opportunity—a place where they could succeed through hard work.

The 3,000-mile (4,800-km) voyage to the United States was costly. Tickets for a couple and their four children to sail from Belfast, Ireland, to New York City cost 21 pounds—equal to $105 at the time. Nonetheless, between 1845 and 1852 about a million Irish people set sail for the East Coast.

The same family could sail to British-held parts of Canada for only 6 pounds, or $30. About 300,000 people took advantage of this lower price. However, many of them were only trying to avoid the steep fare to the United States. After landing in Canada, they traveled south on foot, by stagecoach, or in small boats to cross the border.

The Coffin Ships

The ships that carried Irish Potato Famine emigrants to the New World were often overcrowded, filthy, rickety, and short on food and water. During the transatlantic voyages, which could last up to three months, many lives were lost, and as a result the vessels became known as coffin ships.

About fifty coffin ships sank on the way to North America due to storms and leaks. With about 300 passengers crammed into each ship, that amounted to 15,000 deaths by drowning.

PAYING FOR THE VOYAGE

Poor families sometimes pooled their money and sent several relatives to the United States or another country. Once these family members were settled and working, they were expected to send money back to Ireland so that other relatives could make the trip, too. In this way Irish families moved to a new country little by little.

The following diary entry by a clergyman named B. O'Hara illustrates the passengers' terror during a storm that hit the *Granada* on its way to Boston in 1849:

> The ship bent and bowed and groaned, she heaved and rolled, and although one's heart grew faint as the gloomy horrors of death stared him more and more, yet his attention was arrested by the piercing cries of grief which issued from the hold of the vessel. Here were 250 human beings in a narrow space that was darkened. As each tremendous wave struck the ship it swept across the decks and rushed amongst the poor, terrified passengers. They screamed aloud, frantic in despair that the angry ocean in all its fury had burst in upon them. To quiet them, they were shut in and the hatches closed down but, poor creatures, this augmented their desolation and their cries were loud enough to rise above the storm and reach to heaven.

A killer aboard some coffin ships claimed more lives than the shipwrecks did. Some passengers were ill with typhus or other diseases when they boarded the ships. In the enclosed spaces of the vessels, the diseases spread from person to person and created shipboard epidemics.

The epidemics aboard the coffin ships occurred mostly in 1847 in vessels bound for Canada and the United States. Even after the refugees reached the New World, however, diseases continued to claim lives. Outside the city of Quebec, Canada, on an island known as Grosse-Ile, there was a quarantine station. A quarantine is a period of time when ship passengers can't go ashore until authorities are convinced that they will not spread contagious diseases. Its main purpose is to protect people of the host city and country from being infected by the newcomers.

In spring 1847, the *Ajax*, bound for Canada, departed from Dublin Harbor. Its more than one hundred passengers included a man who kept a journal that was later published as *Robert Whyte's Famine Ship Diary: The Journey of an Irish Coffin Ship*. Here, Whyte describes the outbreak of disease aboard the *Ajax* and the burial at sea of those who died on the voyage:

Sunday, 27 June, 1847

The moaning and raving of the patients kept me awake all night. . . . . It made my heart bleed to listen to the piteous cries of "Water, for God's sake give me some water." Oh! it was horrifying indeed!

Wednesday, 30 June

[P]assing the main hatch, I got a glimpse of the most awful sights I ever beheld. A poor woman was lying upon one of the berths, dying. Her head and face were swollen to almost unnatural size. . . . She had been nearly three weeks ill and suffered exceedingly. . . . Death put a period to her existence shortly after.

Saturday, 3 July

Any idea I ever formed of complete horror was excelled by the stern reality of the frightful picture which the past night presented. The gloom spread around by the impenetrable fog was heightened by the dismal tone of the foghorn, between each sound of which might be heard the cries and ravings of the delirious patients.

Tuesday, 6 July

Two men (brothers) died of dysentery and I was awakened by . . . the mate, who was searching for an old sail to cover the remains with. In about an hour after, they were consigned to the deep, a remaining brother being the solitary mourner. . . . I learned in the afternoon that he was suffering from the same complaint that carried off his brothers.

Friday, 9 July

We now had fifty sick, being nearly one half the whole number of passengers. Some entire families being [ill]. . . . The brother of the two men who died on the sixth followed them to-day. The old sails being all used up, his remains were placed in two meal-sacks [and dropped] into the deep. . . . He left two little orphans. [A] friend of his . . . promised to take care of the children.

According to the usual procedure, quarantine station doctors inspected the ships that arrived at Grosse-Ile. Passengers on ships with no illness aboard were free to continue to their destination. Vessels with diseased passengers were detained, and the sick people were taken to the quarantine hospital on Grosse-Ile.

The problem was that the Grosse-Ile quarantine station wasn't prepared for the huge number of Irish immigrants who arrived in 1847. George Douglas, the physician in charge, had a small staff consisting of about a dozen doctors. There weren't enough doctors to examine the tens of thousands of refugees who arrived in 1847, to separate the sick from the healthy, and to treat those who were ill.

The first Irish immigrant to die on Grosse-Ile in 1847 was four-year-old Ellen Keane, who was admitted to the hospital on May 17 and succumbed to a fever later that day. Over the next few days, ship after ship arrived, and the hospital quickly filled to capacity. As a result, sick people had to remain aboard the coffin ships, where they spread their diseases. By late May, forty ships were being held at anchor near Grosse-Ile in a line

EMIGRANTS & IMMIGRANTS

Two similar words are used to describe people who leave their homelands and move to a new place. People who leave their country are called *emigrants*. From the perspective of the new country, they are *immigrants*. So, those who left Ireland because of the Great Potato Famine were Irish emigrants. Those who reached the United States or Australia were called Irish-American or Irish-Australian immigrants.

2 miles (3.25 km) long. About fifty people per day were dying on the ships, in the hospital, and in emergency sheds and tents hastily established on the island.

Because they were unable to carefully examine all the immigrants who arrived at Grosse-Ile, doctors pronounced many people healthy when in fact they weren't. These people continued on to such Canadian cities as Quebec, Montreal, and Toronto, where they infected thousands of new victims.

Before 1847 ended, 30,000 Irish refugees had died on the coffin ships headed to Canada, at Grosse-Ile, or in various Canadian cities and towns. Another 11,000 died aboard vessels headed to the United States or shortly after their arrival. In all, more than 40,000 Irish refugees died en route or soon after arriving in North America. Had those 40,000 fatalities been the only deaths associated with the Irish Potato Famine, it would have ranked as a major disaster. They are often overlooked, though, because they were dwarfed by the one million fatalities the famine caused in Ireland.

Despite many deaths, about a million and a half Irish men, women, and children arrived safely in the New World. A large majority settled in the United States, where they began new lives.

A ship enters the Australian port of Queenstown. Not only the Irish poor but also wealthy people fled the famine.

THE IRISH DIASPORA

As of 2011, Ireland's population was 6.3 million. Yet worldwide, 75 million people claimed at least partial Irish ancestry. How can there be twelve times as many people of Irish heritage around the world as there are people in Ireland? The answer is that few countries have had as many people depart to live elsewhere as Ireland. The large-scale migration of people from Ireland to other countries is called the Irish Diaspora, meaning the scattering of the Irish people from their original homeland.

Much of the Irish Diaspora took place from 1845 to 1852, during the Great Potato Famine. Although famine victims settled in many lands from Mexico to New Zealand, most moved to the United States, England, Canada, and Australia.

The Irish in Canada

So many Irish people settled in Canada in the late 1840s that the period became known among Canadians as "the time when the Irish came." The newcomers included

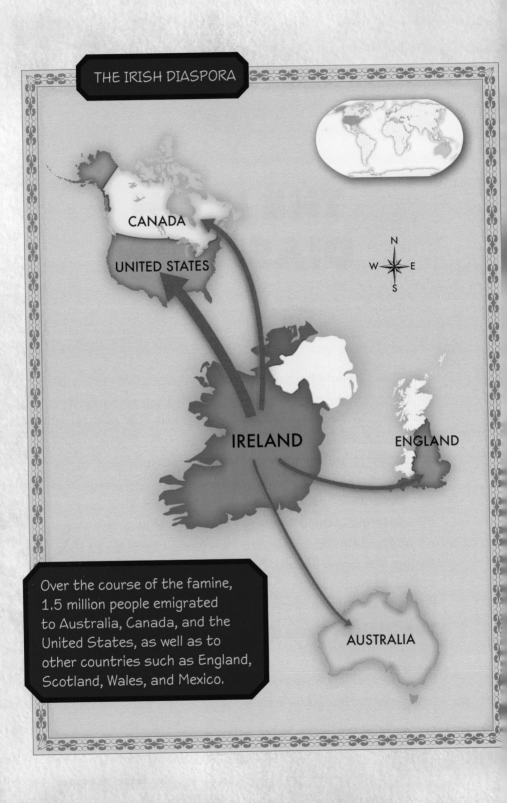

THE IRISH DIASPORA

CANADA

UNITED STATES

IRELAND

ENGLAND

AUSTRALIA

Over the course of the famine, 1.5 million people emigrated to Australia, Canada, and the United States, as well as to other countries such as England, Scotland, Wales, and Mexico.

children whose parents had died on the coffin ships. French-speaking Canadian families adopted many of these Irish boys and girls.

Within a few years, Irish immigrants were one of the largest ethnic groups in nearly every Canadian city. Saint John in the province of New Brunswick became known as Canada's most Irish city. By 1851, nearly half Saint John's population had been born in Ireland. In honor of the Irish people who settled in Montreal, the Irish shamrock (a three-leaved clover) was placed on the city's flag.

Irish people helped build Canada's railroads. Some became farmers or lumberjacks. The Irish also did construction work. Irish immigrants built the Victoria Bridge over the Saint Lawrence River at Montreal. When finished in 1859, it became the world's longest bridge at that time, at 3 miles (4.8 km) across.

Several people whose families arrived during the Irish Potato Famine became important figures in Canadian history. For example, Brian Mulroney's ancestors were poor Irish farmers who moved to Canada to escape the famine in the 1840s. Mulroney served as Canada's prime minister from 1984 to 1993.

The Irish in England

The Irish people who migrated to England during the Great Potato Famine years settled in such cities as London, Birmingham, Manchester, and especially Liverpool. About 170,000 Irish immigrants moved to Liverpool in the first half of 1847 alone. The North End of Liverpool had so many Irish people that it was nicknamed Little Ireland.

The English and Irish had been at odds for centuries, and the arrival of thousands of poor Irish people caused additional resentment. In mid-1847, the English government passed the Poor Removal Act, which allowed local officials to send impoverished Irish people back to Ireland. Under this law, about 70,000 Irish men, women, and children were forced to return to Ireland between 1847 and 1853.

The Irish immigrants who were allowed to remain in England gradually found work. They built railroads and canals. They joined the British army and navy. As the Irish gained acceptance, more of them moved to England. Today, roughly one-quarter of the people in Britain say they are of Irish ancestry.

In 1997, on the 150th anniversary of the Irish Potato Famine, British prime minister Tony Blair did something that no British leader had done before. He apologized to the Irish people. "The Famine . . . has left deep scars," he said. "That one million people died in what was then part of the richest and most powerful nation in the world still causes pain. . . . Those who governed in London at the time failed their people."

The Irish in Australia

The thousands of Irish people who sailed to Australia during the Great Famine arrived at a good time. Gold was discovered in Australia in 1851, and the subsequent gold rush lasted about ten years. Many of the Irish immigrants sought their fortune in Australia's goldfields. Others went to work as fishermen or whalers. Some became farmers.

A memorable episode in Australian history occurred during the Irish Potato Famine. Back in Ireland, large numbers of young people whose parents had died were living in workhouses. In Australia there was a shortage of females, because most of the immigrants who had moved there were men. From 1848 to 1852, about 4,200 orphan girls, ages thirteen to eighteen, were sent from Irish poorhouses to live in Australia. After completing the 10,000-mile (16,000-km) voyage, the girls were hired to work as servants. Many of the

Pépite bienvénue.

Reine des pépites.

In 1851 a veteran of the California Gold Rush discovered gold in Australia. A year later, 95,000 miners settled in New South Wales and Victoria.

young ladies eventually got married and raised large families in Australia.

The Irish in the United States

The Irish people who escaped the Great Potato Famine had been mainly farmers living in the country. Yet in the United States, as many as 90 percent of the refugees settled in Boston, New York, Philadelphia, Chicago, and other cities.

One reason Irish immigrants became city dwellers was that they were poor. City life was less costly than buying and maintaining a farm. Also, like Britain, the United States had strong anti-Catholic sentiment. By gathering in city neighborhoods, the Irish had some protection against bigots.

Establishing themselves in a new country was difficult for the newcomers. Many of them arrived in the United States with no money, no friends, no education, nowhere to live, and no job prospects. Many Americans associated Irish immigrants with disease and poverty. No IRISH NEED APPLY, a nasty slogan informing Irish Americans that they were not wanted for certain jobs, began appearing in store windows and newspaper want ads. At first, Irish refugees could obtain only the least desirable jobs. Men loaded and unloaded cargo ships, did maintenance work, built sewers, and cleaned horse stables. Irish women worked as maids and cooks.

Because of their meager incomes, Irish immigrants often lived crowded together in the poorest neighborhoods. In some cities, homes that had once been single-family dwellings were divided into a dozen apartments, each inhabited by about ten people. A family wanting a room in one of these subdivided homes had to pay a monthly rent of about $5—equal to about $125 today. Many Irish newcomers who couldn't afford that much rent took pieces of wood from junk piles and built shacks in vacant lots.

The overcrowded neighborhoods were breeding grounds for cholera and other diseases. In Boston during the 1840s, 62 percent of Irish American children died before their fifth birthdays. Boston census official Lemuel Shattuck commented that children in the city's Irish neighborhoods seemed to be "born to die." The situation was similar in New York City, where typhus and typhoid fever epidemics killed thousands of people—many of them Irish immigrants—in 1847.

Despite the hardships, the Irish still felt that America was a land of opportunity. People who settled in the United States often sent portions of their salaries back home to help relatives pay for their own voyages across the ocean. Many families back in Ireland were facing life and death situations. "If you knew what hunger we . . . are suffering, . . . you would take us out of this poverty Isle," Mary and Michael Rush of Ireland's County Sligo wrote to Mary's parents in Canada. "For God's sake . . . don't let us die with the hunger."

Although the Irish Potato Famine ended in 1852, more potato crop failures occurred in the late 1800s. Irish people continued to move abroad. Each year between 1852 and 1921, an average of 55,000 people moved from Ireland to the United States.

As their numbers grew, people of Irish heritage joined the mainstream of American life. During the American Civil War (1861–1865), 150,000 Irishmen fought in the Union Army. About 30,000 Irish fought for the Confederate Army. The men of the Irish Brigade, a unit led by County Waterford native Thomas Francis Meagher, fought valiantly at many Civil War battles.

By helping the Union win the war, Irish Americans won the respect of other Americans. Irish immigrants' pursuit of education earned respect as well. Partly because Catholic students suffered discrimination in public schools, the Catholic Church established parochial schools for Irish-

American children. While providing both a general and a religious education, these schools became known for their high standards and strictness.

Between the 1840s and 1900, the Catholic Church also established many excellent colleges for Irish Americans and other Catholics in the United States. They included Boston College in Massachusetts; Catholic University of America in Washington, D.C.; Fordham University in New York City; Seton Hall University in New Jersey; Villanova University in Pennsylvania; DePaul University in Illinois; Marquette University in Wisconsin; and the University of Notre Dame in Indiana. Notre Dame's sports teams were named the Fighting Irish in honor of the soldiers who served with the Irish Brigade in the Civil War.

After the Civil War, Irish Americans rebuilt war-torn towns, worked in factories, mined coal, and opened their own stores. They helped build the Brooklyn Bridge in New York City, as

TWO IRISH CANDIDATES FOR U.S. PRESIDENT

The 2008 U.S. presidential election featured two candidates of Irish heritage. Senator John McCain, who lost the election, is of Northern Irish ancestry. The winner, Barack Obama, is of Irish heritage on his mother's side. In 1850, during the potato famine, one of Obama's ancestors, Fulmuth Kearney, emigrated from County Offaly to the United States.

well as the first coast-to-coast railroad in the United States. Many Irish Americans became policemen and firefighters. By 1870, about half of New York City's police officers were of Irish heritage. Irish Americans with college degrees became priests, teachers, doctors, and lawyers.

Having long been denied the vote in Ireland, Irish Americans relished the right to cast ballots and to run for public office in the United States. They became a powerful force in American politics. For example, John T. Browne, nicknamed the Fighting Irishman, was born in County Limerick at the

The plan to establish an organization of Irish-American policemen—the NYPD Emerald Society—began with a small group of policewomen in 1953.

start of the Great Potato Famine. He moved to Texas, where he served as mayor of Houston from 1892 to 1896. James Michael Curley was born in Boston to poor immigrants from County Galway. He was a high school dropout but educated himself by reading in the public library. In the early 1900s, Curley began a political career that included his serving as mayor of Boston and governor of Massachusetts.

Some Americans believed that the influx of Irish immigrants would be a burden on the nation. Instead, Irish people enriched the nation. In 1963, President John F. Kennedy visited the Emerald Isle. In Dublin he spoke to the Irish parliament about the close bond between the United States and Ireland:

Excited crowds greet President Kennedy during his June 1963 visit to Ireland. During this visit he traveled to his ancestral home in New Ross, County Wexford.

[N]o country contributed more to building my own than your sons and daughters. They came to our shores in a mixture of hope and agony, and I would not underrate the difficulties . . . once they arrived in the United States. They left behind . . . a nation yearning to be free. . . . But today this is no longer the country of hunger and famine that those emigrants left behind. . . . Nor is it any longer a country of persecution—political or religious. It is a free country, and that is why any American [visitor] feels at home.

This poster commemorates "The Cause of Ireland" and Charles Stewart Parnell (center), Irish statesman and nationalist.

FIVE

MEANWHILE, BACK IN IRELAND . . .

As Irish immigrants settled in faraway lands, life gradually improved for famine survivors in Ireland. In 1879, Michael Davitt, Charles Stewart Parnell, and others formed the Irish Land League. One of the league's goals was for tenant farmers to gain ownership of the lands they rented from British landlords. Davitt coined a slogan: "The land of Ireland for the people of Ireland." The members of the Irish Land League fought landlords with both words and weapons. The organization's work reduced rents for farmlands, prevented evictions of families who missed rent payments, and helped many families buy lands they had rented.

By sparking more hatred toward England, the Irish Potato Famine injected life into the battle for Ireland's independence. Starting in the mid-1800s, one Irish revolt against England

MICHAEL DAVITT

Michael Davitt (1846–1906) was born in Straide, a small town in County Mayo, during the Irish Potato Famine. When he was four, his family was evicted from their home for not paying their rent. They moved to England, where Davitt went to work in a cotton mill at age nine. Two years later he lost his right arm after it was mangled in some machinery. Davitt decided to work for change. At age nineteen he joined the Irish Republican Brotherhood, a secret, revolutionary group determined to establish an independent Irish republic. After being caught smuggling weapons for an attack on England, he spent seven and a half years in solitary confinement in prison. Upon his release, he returned to Ireland and organized the Irish Land League. Davitt ended up in jail twice more as he worked to protect the rights of tenant farmers and factory workers. He also wrote books in which he argued for fairer treatment of oppressed groups around the world, such as Jewish people in Russia and the Aborigines in Australia.

followed another. One revolt, called the 1848 Rising, took place during the famine. Later came the Fenian Revolt of 1867 and the Easter Rebellion of 1916. In 1919, people seeking independence created the Irish Republican Army (IRA). In turn, the English established the Black and Tans, an armed police force that fought the IRA in the early 1920s.

For the most part, the powerful British military squashed the Irish revolutionaries. Soldiers shed a great deal of blood in the process. In the Easter Rebellion, about 1,500 people fought, and 450 were killed. Realizing that the revolutionaries would continue fighting until they achieved independence, English lawmakers began to grant Irish demands. In 1921, the Emerald Isle was divided into two countries. The smaller,

Soldiers fight during the Easter Rebellion of 1916. Also known as the Easter Rising, the pivotal event took place on Easter Monday, April 24, 1916.

mainly Protestant, country in the northeast was called Northern Ireland. The southern five-sixths of the island, which was mainly Catholic, became the Irish Free State.

The Irish Free State maintained some ties to England. For example, it had to retain English naval bases and acknowledge the English monarch as chief of state. Leaders of the Irish Free State gradually cut these ties. Then, in late 1948, Irish Free State prime minister John A. Costello introduced to his country's lawmakers a bill that "will end, and end forever, the country's long and tragic association with the British Crown." The bill passed unanimously, and on April 18, 1949, after more than seven centuries of British

THE TROUBLES

Splitting the Emerald Isle into two countries did not end hostilities. Many people in the Irish Free State (later called the Republic of Ireland) were bitter about the division. They wanted one Ireland comprising the entire island. Besides, the Catholics, who were in the minority in Northern Island, felt that the Protestant majority discriminated against them in such areas as jobs and housing. Fighting between Catholics and Protestants in Northern Ireland began in the 1960s and continued for about thirty years. People in Ireland referred to the riots, bombings, and other acts of violence as the Troubles. Nearly four thousand people had been killed by the time the Troubles eased up in the late 1990s. To this day, violence still flares up between Northern Ireland's two groups from time to time.

domination, the Irish Free State's government declared the nation completely independent. They named their new nation the Republic of Ireland.

Meanwhile, agricultural improvements were happening in Ireland. Researchers introduced new varieties of potatoes that stood up better to plant diseases. Farmers also realized the danger of depending too heavily on one crop. They began to produce large amounts of sugar beets, wheat, barley, turnips, oats, beef and dairy cattle, chickens, and sheep.

In recent decades, Irish people have found new ways to earn a living. Manufacturing now employs large numbers of people and brings a great deal of money into the country. Factories produce packaged foods and drinks, clothing, chemicals, pharmaceuticals, metals, glassware, furniture, and computers. Tourism has become another big industry. About a million tourists from the United States alone visit Ireland each

There have been other major famines in various parts of the world since the Irish Potato Famine. A famine brought on by drought struck China from 1876 to 1879. The drought, which claimed up to 13 million lives, may have been the deadliest natural disaster of any type in history. Terrible famines have occurred in the twentieth century in India, Russia, China, Ethiopia, and other African nations.

year. People visit the Emerald Isle to see its castles, gardens, cathedrals, natural wonders, and historic sites. People from many countries where Irish people have settled visit Ireland to see where their ancestors lived.

In 2006, former Republic of Ireland president Mary Robinson spoke on Radio Free Europe about the Irish Potato Famine and the progress her country has made in the years since:

> The Potato Famine in Ireland began in 1845, when the staple crop for the poorest families failed. Those that were strong enough emigrated; some of them died on ships, the coffin ships, and some reached foreign shores. . . . [U]nderstanding the grief of the past that is still there in the present, is really very important. During my seven years as president (1990–1997), we commemorated . . . the terrible Famine, because it was the 150th anniversary. . . . [E]very school had projects; every community remembered. I unveiled so many different monuments, in [Ireland], in Canada, in the United States, Australia. . . .
>
> Now (we have) a more prosperous Ireland. . . . I think that the real key to Ireland's economic success . . . is education. . . . We put a lot of emphasis on that. . . .

MARY ROBINSON, IRELAND'S FIRST WOMAN PRESIDENT

Mary Robinson was born in the town of Ballina in County Mayo in 1944. She studied law at Trinity College in Dublin, which is Ireland's oldest university, and at Harvard University in the United States. At the age of just twenty-five she was elected to the Irish Senate, where she worked for the rights of women and minorities. After twenty years in the senate, she ran for the office of president of the Republic of Ireland—and won. The country's first female president served from 1990 to 1997. Although Robinson may have been Ireland's most popular political leader in history, she resigned a few months early to become United Nations high commissioner for human rights. She felt that the Irish people, having survived the Great Hunger, had a special feeling for the poor and downtrodden of the world.

Lessons for the Future

The Irish Potato Famine was one of the biggest disasters in European history. The scourge killed a million people and drove millions more out of Ireland. It shaped the course of history both in Ireland and in countries where Irish people settled.

Historians still disagree over why and how the famine happened. Was the *Phytophthora infestans* fungus the main culprit, as some claim? Was the Irish people's overreliance on potatoes the leading cause, as others say? How much of a role did Britain's indifference and laissez-faire attitude play in the disaster? Or was the Great Famine the result of all these factors?

Answering these questions isn't just important for history's sake. As the world's population soars, food shortages may threaten many countries in the twenty-first century. Lessons learned from the Irish Potato Famine could help us prevent similar disasters in the future.

TIME LINE

1171—King Henry II of England seizes control of Ireland.

1585-1600—People begin planting potatoes in Ireland.

mid-1600s—British landlords control 80 percent of the land in Ireland.

1695-1725—British parliament passes anti-Catholic laws.

1740-1741—400,000 Irish people die of starvation and disease due to potato crop failure.

1770s—Landlords loyal to England hold about 95 percent of Irish lands.

1798—Theobald Wolfe Tone's rebellion against England fails.

1801—The United Kingdom of Great Britain and Ireland is established; England still dominates Ireland.

1803—Robert Emmet's revolt is crushed.

1829—The Catholic Emancipation Act grants some political rights to Irish Catholics.

1840s—Ireland's population is 9 million. Potatoes are virtually the only food for 3 million people and are a vital part of the diet for another 3 million.

1845—The Irish Potato Famine begins.

1847—Ireland experiences the worst year of the famine.

1852—The Irish Potato Famine ends; a million people have died, and 1.5 million have left Ireland for other nations.

1879—The Irish Land League is founded.

1921—The Emerald Isle is divided into Northern Ireland and the Irish Free State.

1945—The one hundredth anniversary of the beginning of the Irish Potato Famine passes.

1949—The Irish Free State becomes the Republic of Ireland.

1960—Irish American John F. Kennedy is elected first Catholic president of the United States.

1990—Mary Robinson is elected first woman president of the Republic of Ireland.

1995—The 150th anniversary of the start of the Irish Potato Famine passes.

2010—Together, the Republic of Ireland (4.5 million) and Northern Ireland (1.8 million) have 6.3 million people, about 2.7 million less than Ireland's population just before the Irish Potato Famine. The Great Hunger was the main cause of this population loss.

NOTES

All websites were accessed between May and June, 2010.

Introduction

p. 6, par. 1, "'living, walking ghosts . . . '": Asenath Nicholson, *Annals of the Famine in Ireland*, (Dublin: Lilliput Press, 1998), p. 118.

p. 6, par. 2, "'Reader, if you have never seen a starving . . .'": Nicholson, pp. 38–39.

p. 6, sidebar, "'Walls of mud . . .'": Dennis B. Fradin, *The Republic of Ireland*, (Chicago: Children's Press, 1984), p. 41.

p. 7, par. 2, "'We must die of the hunger . . .'": Nicholson, p. 40.

Chapter One

p. 9, par. 1, "People first lived in Ireland . . . ": Fradin, pp. 18–40.

p. 11, sidebar, par. 1, "Potatoes are so closely associated with Ireland . . . ": Redcliffe Salaman, *The History and Social Influence of the Potato*, (Cambridge: Cambridge University Press, 1986), pp. 1–5.

p. 11, sidebar, par. 2, "Explorers returning from the New World . . . ": Salaman, pp. 143–149.

p. 13, par. 5, "Ireland had excellent potato-growing conditions . . . ": Christine Kinealy, *A Death-Dealing Famine: The Great Hunger in Ireland,* (London: Pluto Press, 1997), p. 32.

p. 14, par. 1, "On average, adults in Ireland ate . . . ": E. Margaret Crawford, "Food and Famine," in *The Great Irish Famine*, ed. Cathal Poirteir, (Cork, Ireland: Merceir Press, 1995), p. 60.

p. 15, par. 1, "Between 1800 and 1844 . . . " Salaman, pp. 604–607.

Chapter Two

p. 17, par. 1, "One of the worst disasters . . . ": Salaman, pp. 290–291.

p. 17, par. 3, "We stop the press . . . ": Cecil Woodham-Smith, *The Great Hunger: Ireland 1845–9*, (London: Hamish Hamilton, 1962), p. 40.

p. 18, par. 1, "The answer to Dr. Lindley's question . . . ": James S. Donnelly Jr., *The Great Irish Potato Famine*, (Phoenix Mill, England: Sutton Publishing, 2001), pp. 57–59.

p. 18, par. 3, "'the houses were then demolished . . .'": Woodham-Smith, pp. 71–72.

p. 20, par. 1, "'skeletons, their features sharpened . . .'": Woodham-Smith, p. 158.

p. 20, par. 3, "'A cabin was seen closed . . .'": Nicholson, pp. 117–118.

p. 21, par. 1, "What about the tall man . . . ": Nicholson, pp. 40–41.

p. 22, par. 2, "According to Ireland's 1851 census . . . ": Salaman, p. 304.

p. 22, par. 3, "In the province of Munster . . . ": Brendan O'Cathaoir, *Famine Diary*, (Dublin: Irish Academic Press, 1999), p. 145.

p. 22, par. 4, "Dysentery killed 25,000 people . . . ": Salaman, p. 304.

p. 23, par. 1, "'The Almighty, indeed, sent the potato . . .'": Christine Kinealy, *A Death-Dealing Famine: The Great Hunger in Ireland*, (London: Pluto Press, 1997), p. 6.

p. 23, par. 1, "'the culmination of generations of neglect . . .'": William B. Rogers, "The Great Hunger: Act of God or Acts of Man?" in *Ireland's Great Hunger*, David A. Valone and Christine Kinealy, eds., (Lanham, MD: University Press of America, 2002), pp. 239–240.

p. 24, par. 3, "'Ireland cannot be left . . .'": Kinealy, p. 129.

p. 24, par. 3, "'slowly murdering the peasantry . . .'": Kinealy, p. 130.

p. 24, par. 4, "Laissez-faire is a French . . . ": Woodham-Smith, pp. 54–55.

p. 25, sidebar, "Charles Trevelyan (1807–1886) . . . ": Woodham-Smith, pp. 58–61; "[Sir] Charles Edward Trevelyan,": www.pgil-eirdata.org/html/pgil_datasets/authors/t/Trevelyan,CE/life.htm

p. 26, par. 1, "'We cannot feed the [Irish] . . .'": Rogers, p. 240.

p. 26, par. 3, "'the judgement of God . . .'": Kinealy, p .4.

p. 26, par. 3, "'a direct stroke . . .'": Donnelly, p. 20.

p. 26, par. 4, "Fever hospitals, a key part . . . ": Donnelly, pp. 104–105.

p. 26, par. 5, "'Appalling, awful, heart sickening . . .'": Woodham-Smith, p. 200.

p. 27, par. 2, "In addition to fever hospitals, 130 workhouses. . . ": Donnelly, pp. 103–107.

p. 28, par. 2, "At the workhouse in Bandon . . . ": Woodham-Smith, p. 200.

p. 28, par. 2, "'It was enough to have broken . . .'": O'Cathaoir, p. 145.

p. 29, par. 1,"For instance, the tall road builder earned . . . ": Nicholson, p. 38.

p. 29, par. 2, "Some historians claim that Ireland actually produced . . . ": Kinealy, pp. 5, 66, 79.

p. 31, par. 1, "U.S. organizers held . . . ": Kinealy, pp.106–117.

p. 32, sidebar, "Some people had strange, unscientific theories . . . ": Woodham-Smith, p. 47.

p. 33, par. 1, "By late 1847 . . . ": Kinealy, p. 4.

p. 33, par. 1, "In 1848, the British government . . . ": Rogers, p. 250.

Chapter Three

p. 36, par. 1, "County Limerick residents . . . ": Patricia Lysaght, "Women and the Great Famine," in *The Great Famine and the Irish Diaspora in America*, ed. Arthur Gribben, (Amherst: University of Massachusetts Press, 1999), p. 28.

p. 36, par. 2, "'My father, who was also . . .'": Cathal Poirteir, "Folk Memory and the Famine," in *The Great Irish Famine*, ed. Poirteir, pp. 227–228.

p. 36, par. 3, "Just before the famine began in 1845, Ireland's population was . . . ": Woodham-Smith, p. 31.

p. 36, par. 3 "By 1852, when the famine . . . ": Woodham-Smith, p. 411.

p. 38, par. 1, "Tickets for a couple . . . ": Woodham-Smith, p. 212.

p. 38, par. 4, "About fifty coffin ships sank . . . ": O'Cathaoir, *Famine Diary*, p. xvii.

p. 39, par. 2, "'The ship bent and bowed . . .'": Neil Hogan, "The Famine Beat," in *The Great Famine and the Irish Diaspora in America*, ed. Gribben, p. 171.

p. 40, par. 1, "In spring 1847 the *Ajax* . . . ": James J. Mangan, "Introduction," in *Robert Whyte's 1847 Famine Ship Diary: The Journey of an Irish Coffin Ship*, ed. James J. Mangan, (Cork, Ireland: Mercier Press, 1994), p. 11.

p. 41, par. 1-5 "Sunday, 27 June, 1847 . . . ": Robert Whyte, *Robert Whyte's 1847 Famine Ship Diary*, p. 35; "Wednesday, p. 30 June . . . ": Whyte, pp.36–37; "Saturday, 3 July . . . ": Whyte, p. 38; "Tuesday, 6 July . . . ": Whyte, p. 40; "Friday, 9 July . . . ": Whyte, pp. 41–42.

p. 42, par. 3, "The first Irish immigrant to die . . . ": Michael Quigley, "Grosse Ile," in *The Great Famine and the Irish Diaspora in America*, ed. Gribben, p. 136.

p. 43, par. 2, "Before 1847 ended . . . ": Donnelly, p. 181.

Chapter Four

p. 45, par. 3, "So many Irish people settled in Canada . . . ": "Irish," www.thecanadianencyclopedia.com/PrinterFriendly. cfm?Params=A1ARTA0004055; "History of the Irish in Canada," cisf.concordia.ca/index.php?option=com_content&view=article& id=34&Itemid=51

p. 47, par. 4, "The Irish people who migrated to England . . . ": "Irish Immigration in Liverpool," www.merseyreporter.com/history/historic/irish-immigration.shtml

p. 48, par. 2, "'The Famine . . . has left deep scars . . .'": Kathy Marks, "Blair Issues Apology for Irish Potato Famine," *Independent* June 2, 1997, www.independent.co.uk/news/blair-issues-apology-for-irish-potato-famine-1253790.html

p. 48, par. 3, "The thousands of Irish people who sailed to Australia . . . ": "Discovering Women in Irish History/Australia," www.scoilnet.ie/womeninhistory/content/unit3/Australia.html

p. 50, par. 1, "Yet in the United States . . . ": "The History Place: Irish Potato Famine: Gone to America," www.historyplace.com/worldhistory/famine/america.htm

p. 50, par. 3, "No Irish Need Apply . . . ": "Gone to America," www.historyplace.com/worldhistory/famine/america.htm

p. 50, par. 4, "A family wanting a room . . . ": "Gone to America," www.historyplace.com/worldhistory/famine/america.htm

p. 51, par. 1, "In Boston during the 1840s . . . ": Woodham-Smith, p. 252.

p. 51, par. 1, "'Lemuel Shattuck . . .'": Woodham-Smith, p. 252.

p. 51, par. 2, "'If you knew what hunger we . . .'": Kerby A. Miller and Bruce D. Boling, "The Pauper and the Politician," in *The Great Famine and the Irish Diaspora in America*, ed. Gribben, p. 201.

p. 51, par. 3, "Although the Irish Potato Famine . . . ": Salaman, p. 207.

p. 51, par. 3, "Each year between 1852 and 1921 . . . ": Colm Toibin and Diarmaid Ferriter, *The Irish Famine: A Documentary*, (New York: St. Martin's Press, 2001), p. 171.

p. 51, par. 4, "During the American Civil War . . . ": "Irish-Americans in the Civil War," www.civilwarhome.com/irish.htm

p. 52, sidebar, "In 1850, during the Potato Famine . . . ": "Obama

Irish Roots Include Wigmaker," news.bbc.co.uk/2/hi/uk_news/
northern_ireland/7546326.stm

p. 53, par. 1, "Many Irish Americans . . . ": "Gone to America,"
www.historyplace.com/worldhistory/famine/america.htm

p. 55, par. 1 "'[N]o country contributed more . . .'": "Address
Before the Irish Parliament: President John F. Kennedy," www.
jfklibrary.org/Historical+Resources/Archives/Reference+Desk/
Speeches/JFK/003POF03IrishParliament06281963.htm

Chapter Five

p. 57, par. 1, "In 1879, Michael Davitt . . . ": "Michael
Davitt,"multitext.ucc.ie/d/Michael_Davitt

p. 57, par. 2, "By sparking more hatred . . . ": Fradin, pp. 44–59.

p. 58, sidebar, "Michael Davitt (1846–1906) . . . ": "Life of Michael
Davitt," www.museumsofmayo.com/davitt1.htm; "Michael
Davitt: Mayo's Most Famous Son," www.mayo-ireland.ie/Mayo/
News/ConnTel/CTHistry/MlDavitt.htm

p. 60, sidebar, "Nearly four thousand people had been killed . . . ":
Marie Therese Fay, Mike Morrissey, and Marie Smyth, *Mapping
Troubles-Related Deaths in Northern Ireland 1969–1998*
(extracts), http://cain.ulst.ac.uk/issues/violence/cts/fay98.htm

p. 60, par. 1, "Meanwhile, agricultural improvements . . . ": "Facts
& Figures of Ireland," www.earthyfamily.com/Ir-travel.htm

p. 60, par. 2, "Manufacturing now employs . . . ": "Republic of
Ireland Facts," www.ireland-fun-facts.com/republicofirelandfacts.
html#irish agriculture & industries

p. 61, sidebar, "There have been other major famines . . . ": Dennis
B. Fradin, *Famines*, (Chicago: Children's Press, 1986), p. 47.

p. 61, par. 2, "'The Potato Famine in Ireland . . .'": "EU: Robinson
Sees Strengthening of New Members' Influence, Identity," www.
rferl.org/content/article/1071925.html

p. 62, sidebar, "Mary Robinson was born . . . ": "Biography of
Mary Robinson," www.fulbright.org/node/297; "Mary Robinson
Biography," www.biography.com/articles/Mary-Robinson-9460920

GLOSSARY

colonization—The process of establishing settlements in a foreign land.

commemorated—Remembered or honored with a ceremony.

diaspora—The breaking up and scattering of a nation or people.

discrimination—The mistreatment of people due to a certain characteristic, such as race or religion.

emigrants—People who leave their country to live in another land.

epidemics—Large-scale outbreaks of disease.

famine—A period of widespread and intense hunger and starvation.

fungus—A type of organism that includes mushrooms, molds, and *Phytophthora infestans*, which causes a disease called late blight in potatoes.

immigrants—People who have moved from their homeland to another country.

impoverished—Very poor.

independence—Freedom; ability to stand on one's own.

landlords—Property owners to whom rent is paid.

manufacturing—The making of products.

microorganisms—Small creatures that humans cannot see without a microscope.

parochial schools—Private schools operated by religious groups.

persecution—Poor treatment.

prejudice—A preconceived opinion (usually a dislike) about a group of people.

quarantine—A situation in which people or other animals are kept alone for a certain period of time so that they will not spread diseases.

tenant—A person who rents property from a landlord.

FURTHER INFORMATION

BOOKS

Haugen, Brenda. *The Irish Americans*. Philadelphia: Mason Crest, 2008.

McQuinn, Anna, and Colm McQuinn. *Ireland*. Washington, D.C.: National Geographic, 2008.

O'Neill, Joseph R. *The Irish Potato Famine*. Edina, MN: ABDO, 2009.

WEBSITES

For a detailed description of many aspects of the Irish Potato Famine:

www.historyplace.com/worldhistory/famine/

For a journalist's graphic account of the horrors of the Irish Potato Famine:

www.eyewitnesstohistory.com/irishfamine.htm

For information on Irish immigration to America:

http.library.thinkquest.org/20619/Irish.html

For interactive stories and pictures that lead you through a typical Irish village during the famine:

www.irishpotatofamine.org

BIBLIOGRAPHY

Donnelly, James S. Jr. *The Great Irish Potato Famine.* Phoenix Mill, England: Sutton Publishing, 2001.

Gribben, Arthur, ed. *The Great Famine and the Irish Diaspora in America.* Amherst: University of Massachusetts Press, 1999.

Kinealy, Christine. *A Death-Dealing Famine: The Great Hunger in Ireland.* London: Pluto Press, 1997.

Nicholson, Asenath. *Annals of the Famine in Ireland.* Dublin: Lilliput Press, 1998.

O'Cathaoir, Brendan. *Famine Diary.* Dublin: Irish Academic Press, 1999.

Poirteir, Cathal, ed. *The Great Irish Famine.* Cork, Ireland: Mercier Press, 1995.

Salaman, Redcliffe. *The History and Social Influence of the Potato.* Cambridge: Cambridge University Press, 1986.

Toibin, Colm, and Diarmaid Ferriter. *The Irish Famine: A Documentary.* New York: St. Martin's Press, 2001.

Valone, David A., and Christine Kinealy, eds. *Ireland's Great Hunger: Silence, Memory, and Commemoration.* Lanham, MD: University Press of America, 2002.

Whyte, Robert. *Robert Whyte's 1847 Famine Ship Diary: The Journey of an Irish Coffin Ship,* Edited by James J. Mangan. Cork, Ireland: Mercier Press, 1994.

Woodham-Smith, Cecil. *The Great Hunger: Ireland 1845–9.* London: Hamish Hamilton, 1962.

INDEX

agriculture
  Celtic people and, 9
  during Irish Potato
    Famine, 29–30
  modern Ireland and, 60
  potato farming and, 13–15
Ajax (ship), 40–41
American Indians, 30
*Annals of the Famine in
  Ireland* (Nicholson), 5–7, 20
anti-Catholic prejudice, 24,
  50, 51
Australia, 37, 48, **49**, 50

Black and Tans, 58
Blair, Tony, 48
British Relief Association, 32
Browne, John T., 53–54
burrows and scalps, 18, **19**

Canada, 38, 39, 42–43, 45, 47
Catholicism, 11, 13, 51–52
Celtic crosses, **12**
Celtic people, 9–10
children, 20, 28
China, famine and, 61
Choctaw people, 30
cholera, 22, 36
Christianity
  Catholicism, 11, 13, 51–52
  Saint Patrick and, 9–10
Civil War, U.S., 51
Clarendon, Earl of, 24
Clark, Dennis, 23–24
coffin ships, 37–42, **40**
Costello, John A., 59
costs
  of emigrating, 37, 38

  of relief efforts, 26
crimes, transportation to
  Australia and, 37
crop failures, 14–15
Curley, James Michael, 54

Davitt, Michael, 57, 58
deaths
  in hospitals, 26
  from starvation, 20, 29, 36
  total number of, 36
  while emigrating, 38, 39,
    41, 42, 43
  in workhouses, 27–28
diseases
  coffin ships and, 39, 41,
    42–43
  famines and, 15, 22, 26–27
  immigrant neighborhoods
    and, 51
doctors and medical workers,
  22, 42
Douglas, George, 42
dysentery, 22

Easter Rebellion, 58, **59**
education, 13, 51–52, 61
1848 Rising, 58
emigration, 42, **46**
  to Australia, 37, 48, **49**, 50
  to Canada, 45, 47
  coffin ships and, 37–42
  to England, 37, 47–48
  quarantine stations and,
    42–43
  to the United States, 30–
    31, 37–38, 50–55
employment

Irish immigrants and, 47,
  48, 50, 52–53
modern Ireland and, 60
outdoor relief, 6–7, 28–29
England
  colonization of Ireland and,
    10–11, 13
  emigration to, 37, 47–48
  rebellions against, 57–59,
    60
  relief efforts and, 31–32
  response to Irish Potato
    Famine and, 23–24, 25,
    26, 35
evictions, 11, 18, **19**
exports, of food, 30

families, emigration and, 38,
  51
famines
  emigration and, 51
  Irish Potato Famine, 5,
    17–33
  modern world and, 61
  preventing, 63
Fenian Revolt, 58
fever hospitals, 22, 26–27
food sources, 13–15, 18–19,
  20, 29–30
funguses, 17, 63

Gaelic language, 9
gold rush, Australia, 48, **49**
Grosse-Ile quarantine station,
  39, 42–43

hospitals, 22, **23**, 26–27, 42
housing, 18, **19**, 50–51

immigrants, 42

See also emigration
independence movement,
  57–59
Indian Relief Fund, 32
international aid, Irish Potato
  Famine and, 30–33
Irish Brigade, 51
The Irish Crisis (Trevelyan),
  26
Irish Diaspora, **46**
  Australia and, 48, **49**, 50
  Canada and, 45, 47
  England and, 47–48
  United States and, 50–55
Irish Free State, 59
Irish Land League, 57, 58
Irish Republican Army (IRA),
  58

Kennedy, John F., **54**, 54–55

laissez-faire economics, 24, 63
landlords, 18, 24, 26, 30, 57
land ownership, 11, 13

McCain, John, 52
Meagher, Thomas Francis, 51
Mulroney, Brian, 47

Nicholson, Asenath, 5–7,
  20–21, 28–29
"No Irish Need Apply" signs,
  50
Northern Ireland, 59, 60

Obama, Barack, 52
outdoor relief, 6–7, 28–29

Parnell, Charles Stewart, **56**,
  57

parochial schools, 51–52
Patrick, Saint, 9–10, **10**
Penal Laws, 11, 13
plantation of Ireland, 10–11
political rights, English rule
 and, 13
politics, U.S., 52, 53–54
Poor Removal Act of 1847
 (England), 47–48
population, of Ireland, 14,
 36, 45
potato blight, 5, 17–18, 32,
 63
potatoes, 11, 13–15, **16**
poverty, in Ireland, 6

quarantine stations, 39,
 42–43

railroads, building, 47,
 52–53
Raleigh, Walter, 11
rebellions, against England,
 13, 57–59, 60
relief programs
 English response and, 24,
  25, 26, 35
 hospitals and workhouses,
  26–28
 international aid and, 5–7,
  20–21, 30–33
 outdoor relief, 28–29
religious conflicts, 11, 13, 60
religious groups, relief
 programs and, 32
Republic of Ireland, 59
*Robert Whyte's Famine Ship
 Diary* (Whyte), 40–41
Robinson, Mary, 61, 62, **62**
Rothschild, Lionel de, 32

Russell, John, 26

salaries, for outdoor relief,
 28–29
shipwrecks, 38–39
soup houses, **31**, 32
South America, potatoes
 and, 11
starvation, 15, 20, 22, 29,
 35, 36

Time line, 64–65
Tocqueville, Alexis de, 6
tourism, 60–61
transportation, to Australia,
 37
Trevelyan, Charles, **25**, 25,
 26, 33
the Troubles, 60
Twisleton, Edward, 24
typhus, 22

United States
 emigration to, 30–31,
  37–38
 Irish Diaspora and, 50–55
 relief programs and,
  30–31
universities, Catholic, 52
urban neighborhoods, Irish
 immigrants and, 50–51

woman immigrants, to
 Australia, 48, 50
workhouses, 27–28, 36, 48,
 50
written records, of the
 famine, 19, 20, 35–36, 39,
 40–41

ABOUT THE AUTHOR

Dennis Fradin is the author of 150 books, some of them written with his wife, Judith Bloom Fradin. Their book for Clarion, *The Power of One: Daisy Bates and the Little Rock Nine*, was named a Golden Kite Honor Book. Another of Dennis's well-known books is *Let It Begin Here! Lexington & Concord: First Battles of the American Revolution*, published by Walker. Other books by the Fradins include *Jane Addams: Champion of Democracy* for Clarion and *5,000 Miles to Freedom: Ellen and William Craft's Flight from Slavery* for National Geographic Children's Books. Their latest project for National Geographic is the *Witness to Disaster* series about natural disasters. Dennis's first series for Marshall Cavendish Benchmark was *Turning Points in U.S. History*. A title from that series, *Hurricane Katrina*, was noted as an Honor Book by the Society of School Librarians International. The Fradins also wrote *Money Smart*, a series on financial literacy for kids published by Marshall Cavendish Benchmark. They have three grown children and seven grandchildren.